General Instructic

Optional Bottom

1 Cut one piece 30 holes x 30 holes for bottom and one piece 30 holes x 12 holes for flap.

2 Using matching yarn color and referring to Optional Bottom Assembly diagram, Whipstitch flap to bottom along one edge. Whipstitch opposite edge of bottom to one bottom edge of tissue cover. Overcast unfinished edges.

3 Hot-glue halves of hook-and-loop closure to matching positions on outside of flap and inside of tissue cover.

4 *To close:* Tuck flap between tissue box and cover; press halves of closure together.

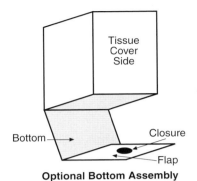

Optional Bottom Assembly

Be Mine

Design by Nancy Dorman

Size: Fits boutique-style tissue box
Skill Level: Beginner

Materials
❏ 2 sheets clear 7-count plastic canvas
❏ Medium weight yarn as listed in color key
❏ 6-strand embroidery floss as listed in color key
❏ 1¼ yards (1.5m) narrow white ruffled lace
❏ Polyester fiberfill
❏ Music box button
❏ #16 tapestry needle
❏ Hot-glue gun *or* craft glue

Stitching Step by Step

1 Cut tissue cover top, four sides and four hearts from plastic canvas according to graphs.

2 Stitch plastic canvas according to graphs, filling in uncoded hearts with red Continental Stitches, and referring to stitch diagram, page 3, to work red Smyrna Cross Stitches on top and sides.

3 Using red yarn throughout, Overcast hearts and opening in top. Work French Knots on sides, wrapping yarn once around needle for each knot.

4 *Embroider hearts using embroidery floss:* Straight Stitch flower stems using green. Using white

throughout, Backstitch lines and lettering; work French Knot flowers, wrapping floss once around needle for each knot.

Assembly

1 Hot-glue lace to edges of hearts on reverse side; let dry.

2 Center a heart on one tissue cover side; using red yarn throughout, tack in place at bottom. Add tacking stitches about halfway up each side, squeezing sides of heart in slightly so that heart puffs out in center. Tuck music box button between heart and tissue cover side; add a little fiberfill to hold button securely. Work tacking stitches up sides and over top to hold heart in place.

3 Tack remaining hearts to tissue cover sides in the same manner, stuffing each heart lightly with fiberfill to match heart with music box button.

4 Referring to diagrams A–D for Binding Stitch, stitch tissue cover sides to one another along corners; Overcast bottom edges. Use Binding Stitch to attach assembled sides to top.

Be Mine Side
29 holes x 37 holes
Cut 4

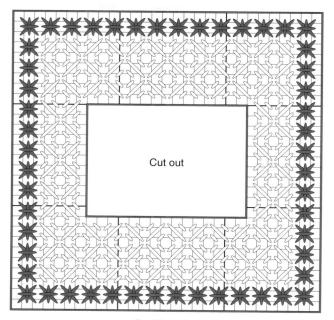

Be Mine Top
29 holes x 29 holes
Cut 1

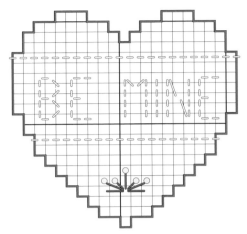

Be Mine Heart
21 holes x 21 holes
Cut 4

COLOR KEY

Yards	Medium Weight Yarn
60 (54.9m)	☐ White
70 (64.1m)	Uncoded areas are red Continental Stitches
	✳ Red Smyrna Cross Stitch
	╱ Red Overcast and Binding Stitch
	● Red (1-wrap) French Knot
	6-Strand Embroidery Floss
10 (9.2m)	╱ White Backstitch
2 (1.9m)	╱ Green Straight Stitch
	○ White (1-wrap) French Knot

Smyrna Cross Stitch
Bring needle up at odd numbers and down at even numbers

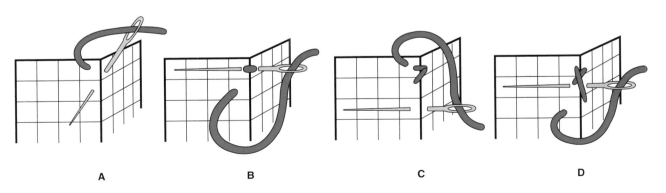

A   B   C   D

Binding Stitch

A Touch of Irish

Design by Gina Woods

Size: Fits boutique-style tissue box
Skill Level: Beginner

Materials

- ❏ 2 sheets clear 7-count plastic canvas
- ❏ Medium weight yarn as listed in color key
- ❏ Kreinik Heavy (#32) Braid as listed in color key
- ❏ Metallic thread as listed in color key
- ❏ DMC 6-strand embroidery floss as listed in color key
- ❏ #16 tapestry needle
- ❏ Hot-glue gun *or* craft glue

Stitching Step by Step

1 Cut tissue cover top and four sides from plastic canvas according to graphs.

2 Work Continental Stitches on sides and top according to graphs, filling in uncoded areas on sides with off-white Continental Stitches and uncoded areas on top with spring green Continental Stitches.

3 Referring to stitch diagram for Extended Cross Stitch, and holding a strand of gold thread with medium purple embroidery floss, work rows of Extended Cross Stitches on sides.

4 Using black embroidery floss, Backstitch and Straight Stitch lettering on top; using medium purple floss, work large Cross Stitches in corners of top.

5 Using a single strand of metallic gold thread throughout, work four long Straight Stitches on each side to outline spring green/off-white areas. Work eight long Straight Stitches on top to outline spring green stitching; Straight Stitch squares around medium purple Cross Stitches.

6 Using dark green yarn, Overcast opening in tissue cover top.

Celtic Crosses

1 Cut 16 Celtic cross pieces from plastic canvas according to graph.

2 Work dark green stitches on Celtic cross pieces according to graph, Overcasting ends as you stitch. Overcast remaining edges of Celtic crosses with gold heavy (#32) braid.

3 Referring to Celtic Knot Assembly diagram and photo throughout, arrange and hot-glue four stitched pieces in a Celtic knot on each side of tissue cover.

Assembly

1 Using dark green yarn throughout, Whipstitch sides to one another along corners.

2 Overcast bottom edges. Whipstitch assembled sides to top.

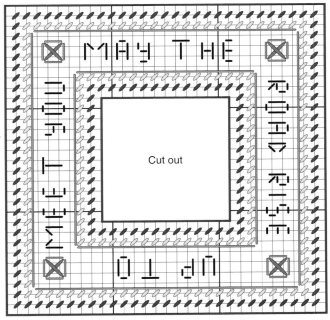

Irish Tissue Cover Top
30 holes x 30 holes
Cut 1

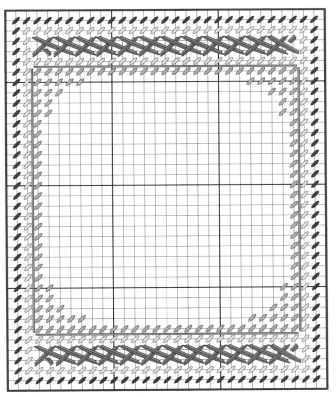

Irish Tissue Cover Side
30 holes x 37 holes
Cut 4

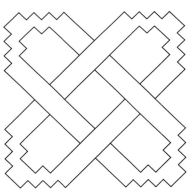

Celtic Knot Assembly

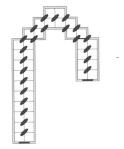

Irish Tissue Cover Celtic Knot
8 holes x 13 holes
Cut 16

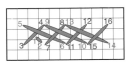

Extended Cross Stitch

COLOR KEY

Yards	Medium Weight Yarn
28 (25.7m)	■ Dark green
20 (18.3m)	☐ Bright green
18 (16.5m)	▨ Spring green
24 (22m)	Uncoded areas on side are off-white Continental Stitches
	Uncoded areas on top are spring green Continental Stitches
	Heavy (#32) Braid
12 (11m)	⁄ Gold #002 Overcast
	Metallic Thread
18 (16.5m)	▨ Gold
	⁄ Gold Straight Stitch
	6-Strand Embroidery Floss
10 (9.2m)	▨ Medium purple #553
3 (2.8m)	⁄ Black #310 Backstitch and Straight Stitch

Color numbers given are for Kreinik Heavy (#32) Braid and DMC 6-strand embroidery floss.

Flower Bunny

Design by Janelle Giese

Size: Fits boutique-style tissue box
Skill Level: Beginner

Materials

- ❏ 1½ sheets clear stiff 7-count plastic canvas
- ❏ Red Heart Classic Art. E267 medium weight yarn as listed in color key
- ❏ Red Heart Super Saver Art. E330 medium weight yarn as listed in color key
- ❏ Red Heart Kids Art. E711 medium weight yarn as listed in color key
- ❏ DMC #3 pearl cotton as listed in color key
- ❏ DMC #5 pearl cotton as listed in color key
- ❏ 5½-inch (14cm) square white felt
- ❏ 3½ yards (3.3m) ⅛-inch-wide (3mm) ivory satin ribbon
- ❏ #16 tapestry needle
- ❏ Hot-glue gun *or* craft glue

Variegated Technique

Refer to these instructions for cutting and stitching with Red Heart Classic country blues #974 yarn.

Cutting variegated yarn—Note that the yarn amount for country blues #974 variegated medium weight yarn is expressed in lengths, not yards. Each length extends from the center of the lightest area to the center of the darkest area on a strand of yarn. To cut these lengths easily, fold the yarn in the center of the lightest area, matching the shading on both sides of the fold (Fig. 1). Cut in the center of the lightest area.

Then fold the yarn in the center of the darkest area, matching the shading on both sides of the fold (Fig. 2). Cut in the center of the darkest area.

The resulting piece—light at one end and dark at the other—is a length of yarn. Cut 42 of these lengths for this project.

Stitching with variegated yarn—Thread the light or dark end (as specified in instructions) on needle. Work rows of stitching in direction indicated by arrows on graph, leaving a 1 to 1½-inch (2.5cm–3.8cm) yarn tail.

Stitching Step by Step

1 Cut tissue cover top, front and three side/back pieces from plastic canvas according to graphs.

2 Work all medium thyme stitches, including Lazy Daisy Stitches, on top, front and side/back pieces. Stitch flower petals and Slanted Gobelin butterflies on side/back pieces. Using eggshell yarn through step 3, Cross Stitch flower centers.

3 Using eggshell yarn throughout, work vertical rows of Continental Stitches on side/back pieces. Referring to stitch diagram for Smyrna Cross Stitch, page 3, work Smyrna Cross Stitches in corners of top, front and side/back pieces.

4 *Variegated rows on front and side/back pieces:* Using the Variegated Technique, thread needle with dark end of one length of country blues yarn. Begin stitching at top of row and stitch to bottom; clip yarn, reserving trimmed piece. Work remaining rows in the same manner, beginning at the top of each row with a new length of yarn, and reserving the trimmed pieces.

5 *Variegated frame rows on top:* Thread needle with lighter end of one trimmed piece. Beginning in one corner in the outer row, stitch toward center of row. Stop stitching when you reach the center of that side of frame. Thread needle with lighter end of another trimmed piece; begin stitching in adjacent corner and stop when you reach lighter end of previous stitching. Continue until outer row is completely stitched, stitching from corner to center, then repeat to stitch inner frame row.

6 *Ribbon borders:* Referring to graph for Corner Detail A, thread a length of ribbon up through upper right corner of tissue cover front and lay it across plastic canvas. Using pale sage yarn, work large Cross Stitches over the ribbon, beginning in the corner and working to the left, and working stitches in order indicated by red numerals on detail graph. At end of row (upper left corner of front), thread ribbon through to reverse side. Continue working pale sage Cross Stitches over ribbon along all borders of front, top and side/back pieces, working stitches in order and in direction indicated. ***Note:*** *The top stitches of all pale sage Cross Stitches should run in the same direction.*

7 *Embroider side/back pieces:* Using dark beige gray #5 pearl cotton, Straight Stitch butterfly bodies and antennae. Using dark blue violet, red copper, deep canary and mauve #3 pearl cotton, Backstitch and Straight Stitch flowers, using color that most closely matches yarn color.

8 Using pale sage yarn, Overcast opening in top.

Bunny

1 Cut bunny from plastic canvas according to graph. Trace around plastic canvas onto felt; cut out just inside traced line.

2 Stitch bunny according to graph, filling uncoded areas with white Continental Stitches. Overcast edges using white, eggshell and tan according to graph.

3 *Eyes:* Referring to Eye Detail graph throughout, outline eyes with eggshell yarn Straight Stitches. Work Straight Stitches using dark beige gray #5 and beige brown #3 pearl cotton. Using 1 ply separated from a length of coffee yarn, work Straight Stitches according to graph; using 2 plies separated from a length of white yarn, add French Knots, wrapping yarn once around needle for each knot.

4 Straight Stitch nose using light raspberry yarn. Straight Stitch ears and mouth using beige brown #3 pearl cotton; Backstitch and Straight Stitch remaining body details using dark beige gray #5 pearl cotton.

5 *Embroider flowers using #3 pearl cotton:* Straight Stitch stems and work Lazy Daisy Stitch leaves using very dark avocado. Work Lazy Daisy Stitch flower petals using dark blue violet, red copper and mauve. Work French Knot flower centers using deep canary, wrapping pearl cotton twice around needle for each knot.

6 Center and hot-glue felt to reverse side of bunny.

Assembly

1 Using pale sage yarn through step 2, Whipstitch sides to one another along corners.

2 Overcast bottom edges. Whipstitch assembled sides to top.

3 Center and hot-glue bunny to front.

Corner Detail A
Upper right corner of sides
Upper right corner of top

Corner Detail B
Lower left corner of sides
Lower left corner of top

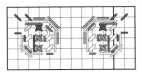

Flower Bunny Eye Detail

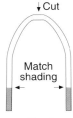

Fig. 1

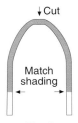

Fig. 2

Flower Bunny Side/Back
31 holes x 37 holes
Cut 3

Flower Bunny Front
31 holes x 37 holes
Cut 1

Continue pattern

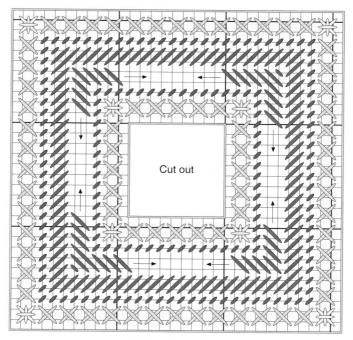

Cut out

Flower Bunny Top
31 holes x 31 holes
Cut 1

COLOR KEY

Lengths	Variegated Medium Weight Yarn
42	■ Country blues #974
Yards	**Medium Weight Yarn**
13 (11.9m)	☐ Eggshell #111
3 (2.8m)	☐ Carrot #256
3 (2.8m)	☐ Tan #334
1 (1m)	■ Coffee #365
17 (15.6m)	■ Medium thyme #406
3 (2.8m)	☐ Lavender #584
21 (19.3m)	☐ Pale sage #622
1 (1m)	☐ Pale rose #755
1 (1m)	■ Claret #762
3 (2.8m)	☐ Light raspberry #774
3 (2.8m)	☐ Yellow #2230
4 (3.7m)	Uncoded areas on bunny are white #1 Continental Stitches
	⁄ White #1 Overcast
	⁄ Eggshell #111 Straight Stitch
	⁄ Light raspberry #774 Straight Stitch
	⁄ Coffee #365 (1-ply) Straight Stitch
	○ White #1 (2-ply, 1-wrap) French Knot
	◑ Medium thyme #406 Lazy Daisy Stitch
	✷ Eggshell #111 Smyrna Cross Stitch
	#3 Pearl Cotton
3 (2.8m)	⁄ Dark blue violet #333 Backstitch and Straight Stitch
1 (1m)	⁄ Beige brown #840 Backstitch and Straight Stitch
3 (2.8m)	⁄ Red copper #919 Backstitch and Straight Stitch
1 (1m)	⁄ Very dark avocado #936 Backstitch and Straight Stitch
2 (1.9m)	⁄ Deep canary #972 Backstitch and Straight Stitch
2 (1.9m)	⁄ Mauve #3687 Backstitch and Straight Stitch
	○ Deep canary #972 (2-wrap) French Knot
	◑ Dark blue violet #333 Lazy Daisy Stitch
	◑ Red copper #919 Lazy Daisy Stitch
	◑ Very dark avocado #936 Lazy Daisy Stitch
	◑ Mauve #3687 Lazy Daisy Stitch
	#5 Pearl Cotton
2 (1.9m)	⁄ Dark beige gray #640 Backstitch and Straight Stitch

Color numbers given are for Red Heart Classic Art. E267, Super Saver Art. E300 and Kids Art. E711 medium weight yarn; and DMC #3 and #5 pearl cotton.

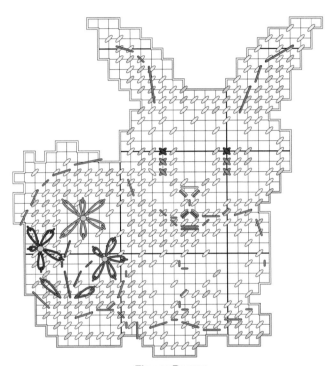

Flower Bunny
29 holes x 33 holes
Cut 1

Country Star

Design by Nancy Dorman

Size: Fits boutique-style tissue box
Skill Level: Beginner

Materials

❏ 2 sheets clear 7-count plastic canvas
❏ Medium weight yarn as listed in color key
❏ #16 tapestry needle
❏ Hot-glue gun *or* craft glue

Stitching Step by Step

1 Cut tissue cover top, four sides, four stars and four hearts from plastic canvas according to graphs.

2 Stitch plastic canvas according to graphs, filling in uncoded stars and uncoded row at bottom of sides with navy Continental Stitches.

3 Overcast hearts and stars with matching colors; Overcast opening in top with maroon.

Assembly

1 Matching colors and pattern of ivory, navy and maroon stripes, Whipstitch sides to one another along corners.

2 Using navy throughout, Overcast bottom edges. Whipstitch assembled sides to top.

3 Referring to photo, center and hot-glue a heart to each star; center and hot-glue star to each side of tissue cover.

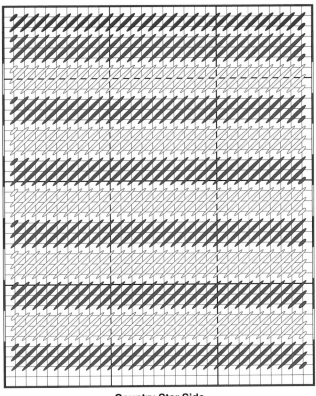

Country Star Side
29 holes x 37 holes
Cut 4

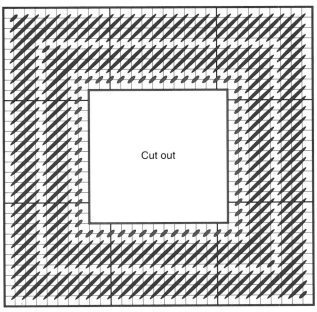

Cut out

Country Star Top
29 holes x 29 holes
Cut 1

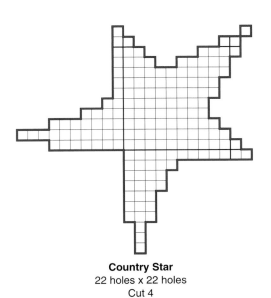

Country Star
22 holes x 22 holes
Cut 4

Country Star Heart
5 holes x 5 holes
Cut 4

COLOR KEY	
Yards	**Medium Weight Yarn**
50 (45.8m)	☐ Ivory
50 (45.8m)	▨ Maroon
50 (45.8m)	■ Navy
	Uncoded areas are navy
	Continental Stitches

Frankie

Design by Sandra Miller Maxfield

Size: Fits boutique-style tissue box
Skill Level: Beginner

Materials

- ❑ 7-count plastic canvas:
    - 2 sheets clear
    - scrap of orange
- ❑ Uniek Needloft plastic canvas yarn as listed in color key
- ❑ #16 tapestry needle
- ❑ Hot-glue gun *or* craft glue

Stitching Step by Step

1 Cut top, four sides, four hair strips, nose, two eyes, one pair of ears and two bolt ends from clear plastic canvas according to graphs. Also cut two pieces 13 holes x 7 holes from clear plastic canvas for bolts; they will remain unstitched.

2 Cut mouth from orange plastic canvas according to graph, carefully cutting away gray shaded areas around bars of plastic canvas. Mouth will remain unstitched.

3 Stitch plastic canvas according to graphs.

4 Overcast bolt ends with gray, ears with bright green, nose with pink and eyes with white and purple according to graph.

5 Using black yarn, Overcast opening in tissue cover top.

Bolts

1 Referring to Bolt Assembly diagram, page 14, and using gray yarn throughout, Whipstitch short edges of one bolt together to form a tube. Overcast ends.

2 Wrap bolt with gray yarn to conceal all plastic canvas; glue yarn ends to secure. Center and hot-glue a bolt end to one end of bolt. Repeat to make a second bolt.

Assembly

1 Using bright green yarn, Whipstitch sides to one another along corners; Overcast bottom edges. Using black yarn, Whipstitch assembled sides to top.

2 Referring to photo throughout and using black yarn, Whipstitch hair strips to one another along corners; Overcast top and bottom edges. Hot-glue hair to tissue cover with top edges even.

3 Hot-glue open ends of bolts to opposite sides of tissue cover just below hair and nearly even with front edge. Hot-glue edges of ears between arrows to tissue cover sides, positioning ears 2¾ inches (7cm) from bottom edge and 1¼ inches (3.2cm) from front edge.

4 Hot-glue eyes, nose and mouth to front of tissue cover.

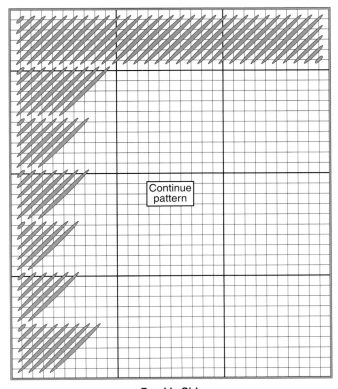

Frankie Side
30 holes x 36 holes
Cut 4 from clear

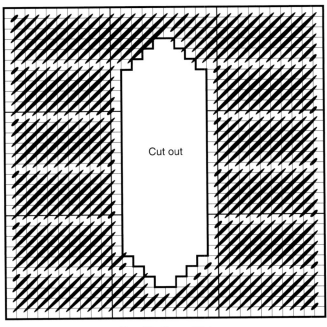

Cut out

Frankie Cover Top
30 holes x 30 holes
Cut 1 from clear

COLOR KEY	
Yards	**Plastic Canvas Yarn**
35 (32.1m)	■ Black #00
3 (2.8m)	▨ Pink #07
10 (9.2m)	▨ Gray #38
1 (1m)	☐ White #41
135 (123.5m)	▨ Bright green #61
3 (2.8m)	▨ Bright purple #64
Color numbers given are for Uniek Needloft plastic canvas yarn.	

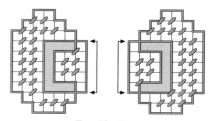

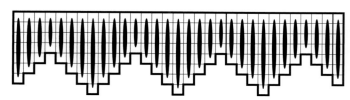

Frankie Ears
7 holes x 10 holes
Cut 1 pair from clear,
cutting away gray areas

Frankie Hair
31 holes x 8 holes
Cut 4 from clear

Frankie Eye
7 holes x 6 holes
Cut 2 from clear

Frankie Bolt End
7 holes x 7 holes
Cut 2 from clear,
cutting away gray area

Frankie Mouth
20 holes x 4 holes
Cut 1 from orange,
cutting away gray areas

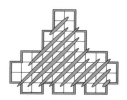

Frankie Nose
10 holes x 8 holes
Cut 1 from clear

Bolt Assembly Diagram

COLOR KEY	
Yards	**Plastic Canvas Yarn**
35 (32.1m)	■ Black #00
3 (2.8m)	■ Pink #07
10 (9.2m)	■ Gray #38
1 (1m)	□ White #41
135 (123.5m)	■ Bright green #61
3 (2.8m)	■ Bright purple #64
Color numbers given are for Uniek Needloft plastic canvas yarn.	

Thanksgiving Gobbler

Design by Michele Wilcox

Size: Fits boutique-style tissue box
Skill Level: Beginner

Materials
- ❑ 2 sheets clear 7-count plastic canvas
- ❑ Uniek Needloft plastic canvas yarn as listed in color key
- ❑ 6-strand embroidery floss as listed in color key
- ❑ #16 tapestry needle
- ❑ Hot-glue gun *or* craft glue

Stitching Step by Step

1 Cut top, four sides, tail feathers, body and two wings from plastic canvas according to graphs.

2 Stitch plastic canvas according to graphs, reversing one wing before stitching, and filling in uncoded areas on body with beige Continental Stitches.

3 Overcast wings with red, tail feathers with cinnamon and body with beige and pumpkin according to graph.

4 Using black embroidery floss, Straight Stitch gobbler's eyebrows and work French Knot eyes, wrapping floss once around needle for each knot.

5 Using pumpkin yarn, Overcast opening in tissue cover top.

Assembly

1 Using pumpkin yarn throughout, Whipstitch sides to one another along corners. Overcast bottom edges. Whipstitch assembled sides to top.

2 Referring to photo, hot-glue wings to reverse side of body. Hot-glue body and wings to right side of tail feathers, bottom edges even. Center and hot-glue tail feathers to one side of tissue cover, bottom edges even.

Gobbler Tissue Cover Side
30 holes x 36 holes
Cut 4

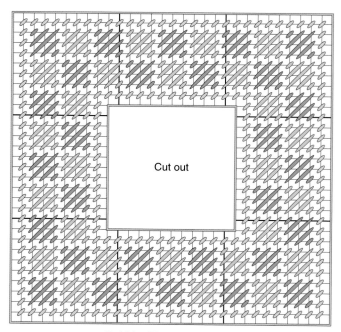

Cut out

Gobbler Tissue Cover Top
30 holes x 30 holes
Cut 1

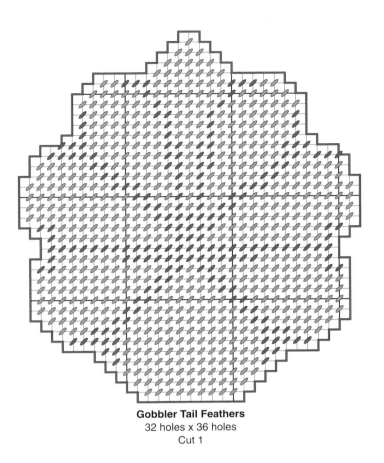

Gobbler Tail Feathers
32 holes x 36 holes
Cut 1

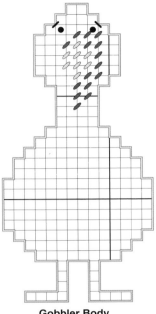

Gobbler Body
14 holes x 29 holes
Cut 1

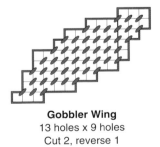

Gobbler Wing
13 holes x 9 holes
Cut 2, reverse 1

COLOR KEY

Yards	Plastic Canvas Yarn
4 (3.7m)	■ Red #01
60 (54.9m)	▨ Rust #09
42 (38.5m)	☐ Pumpkin #12
10 (9.2m)	■ Cinnamon #14
54 (49.5m)	☐ Beige #40

Uncoded areas on body are
beige #40 Continental Stitches

6-Strand Embroidery Floss

1 (1m)	╱ Black Straight Stitch
	● Black (1-wrap) French Knot

Color numbers given are for Uniek Needloft plastic
canvas yarn.

The Gift

Design by Betty Hansen

Size: Fits boutique-style tissue box
Skill Level: Beginner

Materials

- ❑ 2 sheets clear 7-count plastic canvas
- ❑ Medium weight yarn as listed in color key
- ❑ Light weight yarn as listed in color key
- ❑ Metallic yarn as listed in color key
- ❑ Green #3 pearl cotton
- ❑ 92 (6mm) metallic gold beads
- ❑ Tapestry needles: #16, #18

Stitching Step by Step

1 Cut tissue cover top, four sides and four bow strips from plastic canvas according to graphs.

2 Stitch plastic canvas according to graphs.

3 When background stitching is complete, attach gold beads to top, sides and bow strips using #18 needle and #3 pearl cotton.

4 Using metallic gold yarn, Overcast bow strips between black dots, Overcasting long edges and going around bottom corners to add a single Overcast stitch on each end of bottom edge.

Assembly

1 Referring to photo throughout, Whipstitch top edge of strip (between arrows) to one side of cutout opening in top (between arrows) using Christmas green glitter and metallic gold yarn. Repeat to Whipstitch top edge of remaining bow strips to remaining edges of opening. Using red yarn, Overcast unfinished edges of cutout opening.

2 Bend each bow strip over and, using Christmas green glitter and metallic gold yarns, Whipstitch bottom edge to tissue cover top where indicated by blue lines on top graph.

3 Using red yarn, Whipstitch tissue cover sides to one another along corners.

4 Using Christmas green glitter, red and metallic gold yarns throughout, Overcast bottom edges of assembled sides; Whipstitch assembled sides to top.

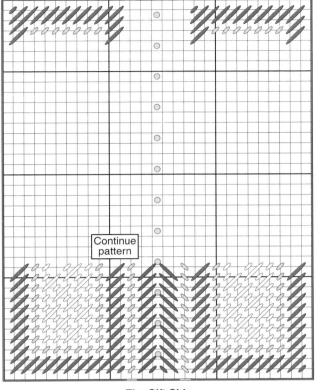

The Gift Side
29 holes x 37 holes
Cut 4

Whipstitch to inside
edge on top

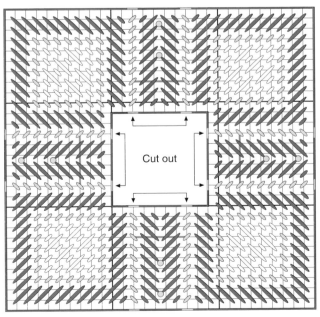

Cut out

The Gift Top
29 holes x 29 holes
Cut 1

COLOR KEY	
Yards	**Medium Weight Yarn**
30 (27.5m)	■ Christmas green glitter
25 (22.9m)	■ Red
	Light Weight Yarn
25 (22.9m)	☐ White pompadour
	Metallic Yarn
15 (13.8m)	☐ Gold
	◉ Attach gold bead

The Gift Bow Strip
5 holes x 34 holes
Cut 4

Deck the Halls Snowman

Design by Nancy Dorman

Size: Fits boutique-style tissue box
Skill Level: Beginner

Materials

- ❏ 2½ sheets clear 7-count plastic canvas
- ❏ Medium weight yarn as listed in color key
- ❏ 25mm Rainbow Gallery Plastic Canvas 10 Metallic Needlepoint Yarn as listed in color key
- ❏ 6-strand embroidery floss as listed in color key
- ❏ 9 inches (22.9cm) ⅛-inch-wide (3mm) green satin ribbon
- ❏ 15 (5-inch/12.7cm) lengths ¹⁄₁₆-inch-wide (1.5mm) maroon satin ribbon
- ❏ 15 (4mm) white pearl beads
- ❏ 13 gold confetti stars
- ❏ Orange hors d'oeuvre pick
- ❏ Hand-sewing needle and dark green thread
- ❏ #16 tapestry needle
- ❏ Hot-glue gun or craft glue

Project Note

Depending on size of tissue box, this topper may fit very snugly.

Stitching Step by Step

1 Cut tissue cover top and four sides from plastic canvas according to graphs.

2 Stitch plastic canvas according to graphs. Using green yarn, Overcast opening in top.

Snowman Motif

1 Cut snowman motif from plastic canvas according to graph.

2 Stitch snowman motif according to graph, filling in uncoded areas on white background on snowman with white Continental Stitches, and uncoded areas on green background on Christmas tree with green Continental Stitches. Overcast edges using white, black, maroon and green medium weight yarn and gold metallic needlepoint yarn according to graph.

3 *Embroider snowman:* Straight Stitch greenery on hat using green embroidery floss. Backstitch vest using 2 plies separated from a length of black yarn. Work French Knot buttons on hat and vest using gold metallic

needlepoint yarn, and French Knot eyes and mouth using a full strand of black yarn, wrapping yarn once around needle for each knot.

4 *Nose:* Referring to photo throughout, clip end from orange hors d'oeuvre pick; hot-glue blunt end to snowman's face where indicated.

5 *Bow tie:* Tie green ribbon in a bow; glue to snowman where indicated.

6 *Tree garland:* Using gold metallic needlepoint yarn, Straight Stitch end of garland across snowman as shown. Lay metallic yarn across tree as shown and secure with tiny Couching Stitches.

7 *Tree ornaments:* Work maroon French Knots on tree where indicated, wrapping yarn once around needle for each knot. Using sewing needle and dark green thread, stitch pearl beads to tree where indicated. Tie maroon ribbon lengths in tiny bows, trimming ends; glue bows and gold stars to tree where indicated.

Assembly

1 Using green yarn throughout and referring to diagrams A–D for Binding Stitch, page 3, stitch tissue cover sides to one another along corners.

2 Overcast bottom edges. Use Binding Stitch to attach assembled sides to top.

3 Center and hot-glue snowman motif to one side of tissue topper with bottom edges even.

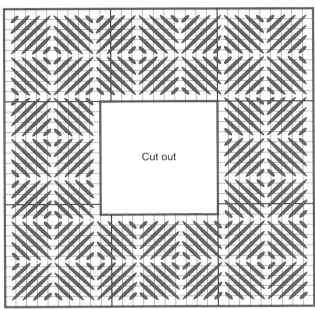

Deck the Halls Snowman Top
29 holes x 29 holes
Cut 1

COLOR KEY	
Yards	**Medium Weight Yarn**
120 (110m)	■ Green
12 (11m)	■ Maroon
6 (5.5m)	■ Black
1 (1m)	□ Gray
	Uncoded areas on green background are green Continental Stitches
20 (18.3m)	Uncoded areas on white background are white Continental Stitches
	⁄ White Overcast
	✓ Black (2-ply) Backstitch
	● Maroon (1-wrap) French Knot
	● Black (1-wrap) French Knot
	Metallic Needlepoint Yarn
5 (4.6m)	▢ Gold #PM51
	⁄ Gold #PM51 Straight Stitch and Couching Stitch
	○ Gold #PM51 (1-wrap) French Knot
	6-Strand Embroidery Floss
1 (1m)	⁄ Green Straight Stitch
	● Attach white pearl bead
	● Attach green ribbon bow
	● Attach maroon ribbon bow
	○ Attach gold star
	○ Attach nose
Color number given is for Rainbow Gallery Plastic Canvas 10 Metallic Needlepoint Yarn.	

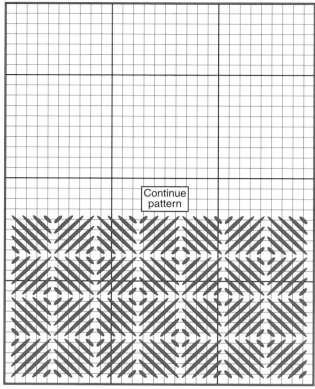

Continue
pattern

Deck the Halls Snowman Side
29 holes x 37 holes
Cut 4

COLOR KEY	
Yards	**Medium Weight Yarn**
120 (110m)	■ Green
12 (11m)	■ Maroon
6 (5.5m)	■ Black
1 (1m)	▫ Gray
	Uncoded areas on green background are green Continental Stitches
20 (18.3m)	Uncoded areas on white background are white Continental Stitches
	⁄ White Overcast
	✔ Black (2-ply) Backstitch
	● Maroon (1-wrap) French Knot
	● Black (1-wrap) French Knot
	Metallic Needlepoint Yarn
5 (4.6m)	▫ Gold #PM51
	⁄ Gold #PM51 Straight Stitch and Couching Stitch
	◦ Gold #PM51 (1-wrap) French Knot
	6-Strand Embroidery Floss
1 (1m)	⁄ Green Straight Stitch
	● Attach white pearl bead
	● Attach green ribbon bow
	◦ Attach maroon ribbon bow
	○ Attach gold star
	○ Attach nose

Color number given is for Rainbow Gallery Plastic Canvas 10 Metallic Needlepoint Yarn.

Deck the Halls Snowman Motif
64 holes x 71 holes
Cut 1

The full line of The Needlecraft Shop
products is carried by Annie's Attic catalog.
TOLL-FREE ORDER LINE
or to request a free catalog
(800) 582-6643
Customer Service
(800) 449-0440
Visit AnniesAttic.com

We have made every effort to ensure the accuracy
and completeness of these instructions. We cannot,
however, be responsible for human error, typographical
mistakes or variations in individual work.

ISBN: 978-1-57367-324-2

Printed in USA

1 2 3 4 5 6 7 8 9

Getting Started

Before You Cut

Buy one brand of canvas for each entire project as brands can differ slightly in the distance between bars. Count holes carefully from the graph before you cut, using the bolder lines that show each 10 holes. These 10-count lines begin in the lower left corner of each graph to make counting easier. Mark canvas before cutting; then remove all marks completely before stitching. If the piece is cut in a rectangular or square shape and is either not worked, or worked with only one color and one type of stitch, the graph is not included in the pattern. Instead, the cutting and stitching instructions are given in the general instructions or with the individual project instructions.

Covering the Canvas

Bring needle up from back of work, leaving a short length of yarn on back of canvas; work over short length to secure. To end a thread, weave needle and thread through the wrong side of your last few stitches; clip. Follow the numbers on the small graphs beside each stitch illustration; bring your needle up from the back of the work on odd numbers and down through the front of the work on even numbers. Work embroidery stitches last, after the canvas has been completely covered by the needlepoint stitches.

Shopping for Supplies

For supplies, first shop your local craft and needlework stores. Some supplies may be found in fabric, hardware and discount stores. If you are unable to find the supplies you need, please call Annie's Attic at (800) 582-6643 to request a free catalog that sells plastic canvas supplies.

Basic Stitches

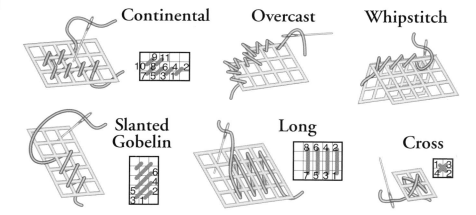

Continental · Overcast · Whipstitch · Slanted Gobelin · Long · Cross

Embroidery Stitches

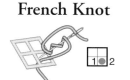
French Knot

Lazy Daisy

Backstitch

Straight

METRIC KEY:
millimeters = (mm)
centimeters = (cm)
meters = (m)
grams = (g)